WIND TO FLIGHT

Design   David West
                      Children's Book Design
Editor   Margaret Fagan
Editorial planning Clark Robinson Limited
Researcher   Cecilia Weston-Baker
Illustrators   Alex Pang
                      Galina Zolfaghari
Consultant   Alan Morton Ph.D.
                      Science Museum, London

© Aladdin Books 1989
Designed and produced by
Aladdin Books Ltd
70 Old Compton Street
London W1

First published in the
United States in 1989 by
Gloucester Press
387 Park Avenue South
New York, NY 10016

Printed in Belgium

Library of Congress Cataloging-in-Publication Data

Lafferty, Peter
    Wind to flight / Peter Lafferty
       p.   cm.—(Hands on science)
    Includes index
    Summary: Examines the nature of wind and how it is used by seeds,
clouds, birds, insects, and flying machines. Includes experiments
and projects throughout.
    ISBN 0-531-17166-3
    1. Winds—Juvenile literature.   2. Winds—Experiments—Juvenile
literature.   3. Convection: Meteorology:—Juvenile literature.
4. Flying-machines—Juvenile literature.   [1. Winds.   2. Winds—
Experiments.   3. Experiments.]   I. Title.   II. Series.
QC931.9.C52   1989
551.5'17—dc20   89-31566
                                                        CIP
                                                          AC

HANDS · ON · SCIENCE

WIND TO FLIGHT

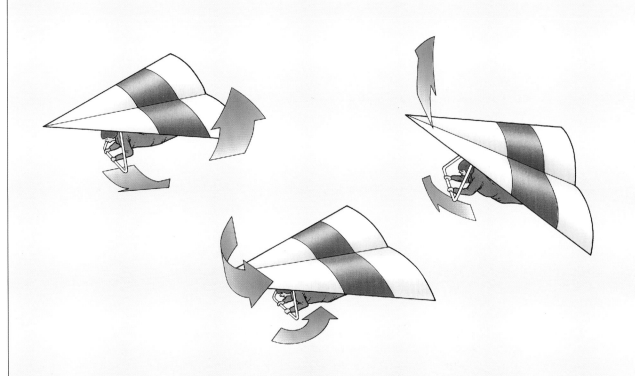

ACADEMY LIBRARY

GLOUCESTER PRESS
New York · London · Toronto · Sydney

Contents

This book is about the movements of the air — or wind. It explains how we use the wind in machines such as windmills and how it can be used to push sailboats along. The book also looks at how animals fly or glide through the air and it ends with a look at the technology of powered flight.

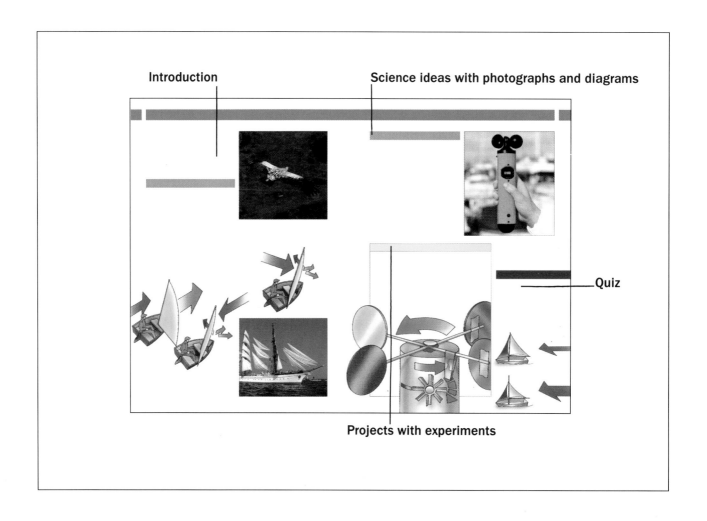

Introduction

Science ideas with photographs and diagrams

Quiz

Projects with experiments

Introduction

The Earth on which we live is surrounded by a layer of air called the atmosphere. This layer extends for about 800 km (500 miles) into space. It is held in place by the Earth's gravity. Most of the air lies close to the Earth's surface. At a height of 5,500 m (18,000ft) the atmosphere is so thin that a person cannot breathe easily without a supply of oxygen. About half the atmosphere lies below this height. Above this height, the amount of air continues to decrease with height until it hardly exists.

As well as providing air to breathe, the atmosphere acts as a blanket for the Earth, making our planet a warm and comfortable place to live. The heat coming from the Sun causes winds, or air movements, in the atmosphere. Sometimes these winds are violent, and full of energy. They can cause damage, but they can be a source of power, and are used to generate electricity, push sailing ships along, and to help aircraft to fly.

A hang glider flies along air currents

Although we do not notice it, the air above us is really quite heavy, and exerts a pressure on the Earth. However, the pressure of the air is not the same all over. The differences in air pressure are caused by differences in temperature. Cold areas tend to have high pressure. Warm areas have low pressure.

WHAT ARE WINDS?

Warm air is lighter and less dense than cold air. Because of this, warm air rises, leaving behind an area of low pressure, called a depression. Cold air sinks downwards in the atmosphere, creating an area of high pressure, called an anticyclone. Winds are caused by air flowing from areas of high pressure to areas of low pressure. The situation is complicated by the rotation of the Earth. This causes winds to blow outwards from the center of an anticyclone in a circular clockwise movement in the northern hemisphere, and in a counterclockwise direction in the southern hemisphere.

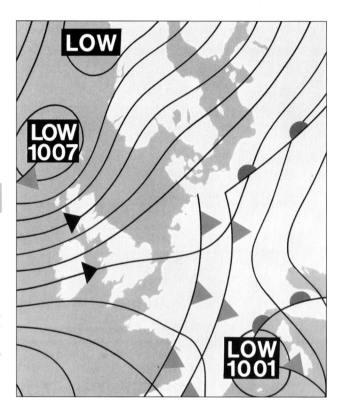

▲ A weather map has lines called isobars drawn on it. They join places with equal air pressure. When the isobars are close together, the winds will be very strong.

WORLD WIND PATTERNS

Where the Earth is hottest — at the Equator — air rises and creates a low pressure region called the doldrums. The air that rises from the doldrums travels away from the Equator and falls when it cools. This creates areas of high pressure known as the horse latitudes. The air that falls in the horse latitudes travels towards the Equator, causing winds called the trade winds. In addition, there is also falling air in the Arctic and Antarctic because these areas are so cold. This creates high pressure areas at the poles, with winds blowing toward the Equator. These winds are called the polar winds. In between the polar winds and the trade winds, there is a belt of winds called the westerlies. These blow from the horse latitudes to the poles.

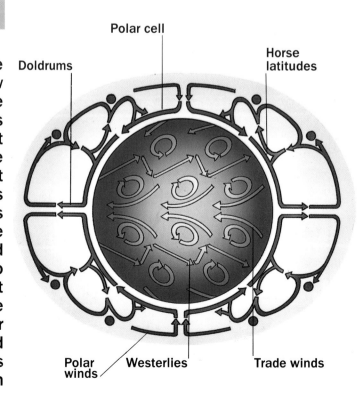

Doldrums

Polar cell

Horse latitudes

Polar winds

Westerlies

Trade winds

GIANT STORMS

Violent storms of whirling wind and rain can start over the seas near the Equator. These storms are called hurricanes when they take place over the Atlantic Ocean, cyclones in the Indian Ocean and typhoons in the Pacific Ocean. Cyclones and hurricanes are very strong winds circling round an area of low pressure. Some cyclones may be 500 km (300 miles) across, with winds blowing at more than 200 km/h (120 mph). A tornado is a funnel-shaped storm that is usually about 100 m (300 ft) across. The air in its centre whirls around at over 600 km/h (360 mph). The low pressure in the center of a tornado can make buildings explode like pricked balloons.

▶ A tornado, or "twister," can suck up everything in its path and cause terrible damage.

MAKE A WIND VANE

Make the vane by taping triangular pieces of cardboard to the ends of a strong plastic drinking straw.

Attach the vane to a rubber-topped pencil using a pin through the center of the straw. Make sure it can turn freely.

Use modeling clay to hold a cardboard tube to a wooden base. Place clay inside the tube to hold the pencil steady.

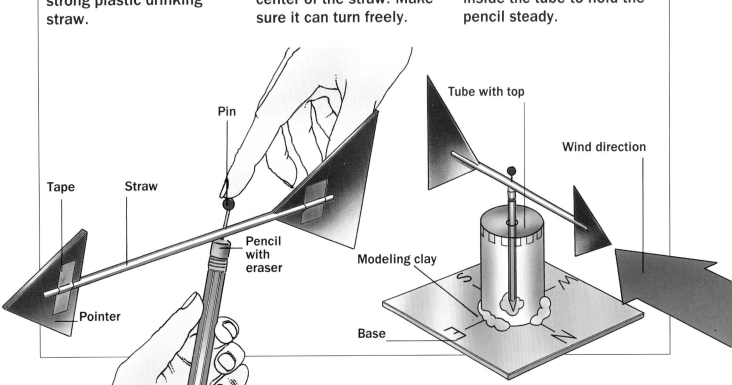

Tape Straw

Pin

Pencil with eraser

Pointer

Tube with top

Wind direction

Modeling clay

Base

The windmill is an ancient source of power. In the year 650, the Persians used windmills to grind corn. By 1200 windmills in Europe pumped water, ground corn and drove machinery. Today windmills make electricity without producing pollution.

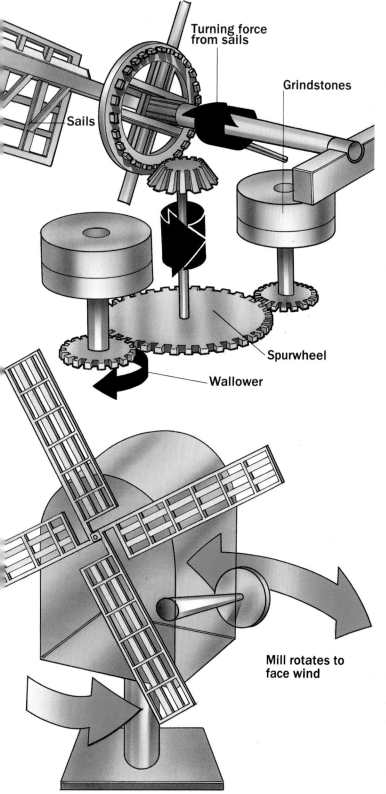

Turning force from sails

Grindstones

Sails

Spurwheel

Wallower

Mill rotates to face wind

▲ Windmills are used to pump water from the low-lying areas in the Netherlands. The largest Dutch windmill, in Maasland, has sails measuring 29 m (95 ft) from tip to tip.

THE WINDMILL

There are two types of traditional windmill. The first type is the post mill, which is turned by hand around a post to face into the wind. The second type is the tower mill which has a revolving turret on top of a tall tower. There is a device, called a fantail, attached to the turret which keeps the sails pointing into the wind. The angle of the wooden sails can be adjusted to extract as much power as possible from the wind. Inside the windmill, the sails turn a drivewheel. The drivewheel is connected to the grindstones, using gears and cogs. The moving grindstones press against two upper fixed stones. The grain is fed to the stones through hoppers in the upper grindstones.

MODERN WINDMILLS

There are several different designs for a large, wind-driven electric generator. Some designs look like large versions of the normal windmill. Often, there are only two giant blades, shaped like the propellers of an airplane. Another design consists of two flexible metal strips connected to an upright pole at the top and bottom. This design catches the wind whatever direction it is blowing in.

▲ Rows of windmills are used to generate electricity in a remote area.

◄ Windmills can be designed with many blades to catch the wind efficiently.

MAKE A WINDMILL AND HAMMER

To make a simple windmill, cut a thin cardboard square about two-thirds of the way along the diagonals. Fold the corners into the center as shown in the diagram. Push a pin through the center and into one end of the stick. Push the straw through holes in the box as shown and insert the stick. Cut a cam and a hammer from the thick cardboard. Attach the cam to the end of the stick. Fix the hammer to the side of the box, using a paper fastener. Face your windmill into the wind.

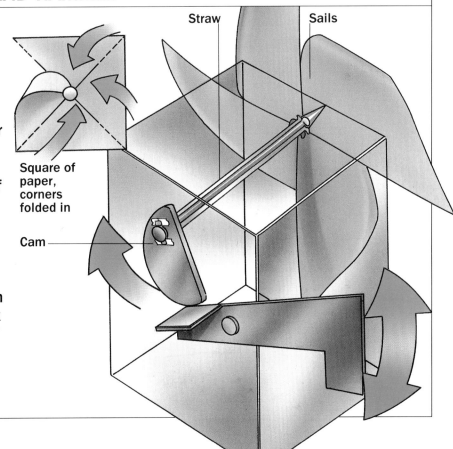

Straw

Sails

Square of paper, corners folded in

Cam

About 5,000 years ago, the Egyptians invented the sail and used the wind to push their boats along. For many centuries, sailing ships ruled the seas. However, after the first boat powered by a steam engine was built in 1783 by the Marquis de Jouffroy d'Abbans, sailing ships became less important.

HOW SAILS WORK

A sailboat can move in any direction, no matter where the wind comes from. This is possible because the sail can catch the wind at any angle. When the wind is directly behind the boat, the sail is held at right angles to the wind. To move in other directions, the sail is held at different angles so that part of the force on the sail pushes the boat in the direction it wants to travel. To move into the wind, the sail is held edge-on to it. Water resistance on the keel of the boat, called the heeling force, helps the sail move the boat in the right direction.

▲ Birds like this eagle can soar to great heights without flapping their wings. They are lifted by air currents.

Sailing across the wind

Heeling force

Wind

Thrust

Force from sail

Sailing before the wind

Force from sail/thrust

Wind

Wind

Heeling force

Thrust

Force from sail

Sailing into the wind

► By changing the position of the sails, boats can sail before and into the wind and can easily change direction.

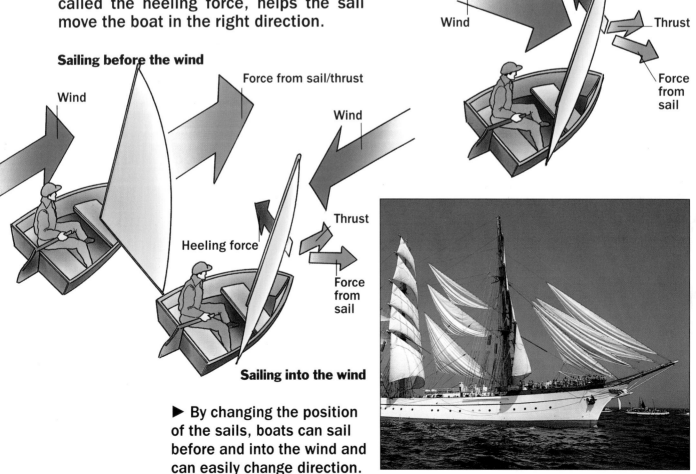

MEASURING THE WIND

The strengths of winds are described using a scale called the Beaufort scale. This scale was developed in 1805 by a British admiral, Francis Beaufort. Wind strength is measured on a scale of 0 to 12. On the Beaufort scale, a calm day is indicated by 0, a gentle breeze is 3, a strong breeze is 6, a strong gale is 9, and a hurricane is 12. To measure wind speed exactly an instrument called an anemometer is used. Some anemometers can measure the direction and the speed of the wind at the same time. They look like small airplanes placed on top of a pole. Other anemometers look like whirling cups on the top of a high post.

MAKE YOUR OWN WIND METER

Fix cardboard disks to strong drinking straws. The straws should be taped together at right angles and fixed to the top of a tube so they can turn easily.

Fix a cardboard paddle wheel to the side of the tube and a cardboard tag to one straw. Make a reference mark on the tube, and number each paddle on the wheel.

▲ A rotating cup anemometer is used at airports and weather stations. The wind speed is measured by turning the trimming wheel.

QUIZ

Why do sailing boats use smaller sails in very strong winds? Do you think that the force produced by the wind on the sails depends upon the size of the sails? What else does the wind force depend upon?

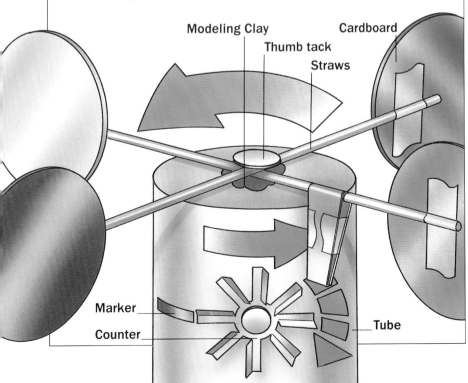

Modeling Clay
Thumb tack
Straws
Cardboard
Marker
Counter
Tube

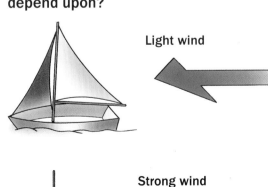

Light wind

Strong wind

When an object moves through the air, the air slows it down. This is because the air rubs against the object, producing a slowing force called "drag," or air resistance. Engineers try to reduce drag by producing sleek designs. In nature, the fastest animals are those with the right shape to reduce drag.

STREAMLINING

A streamlined object has a sleek shape so that air flows smoothly over it. If you tie paper ribbons to a fan, and blow the fan at a round balloon, the ribbons will show that the air moves smoothly around the balloon. The balloon is streamlined. If you hold a flat object, such as a book, facing the airflow, the ribbons show that the airflow is not smooth. Automobile designers see if their designs are streamlined by placing a model of a new car in a wind tunnel. Inside the tunnel, huge fans blow air over the car. Small ribbons attached to the model show the airflow over the car.

▲ A diving bird folds its wings back to make a streamlined shape. This lets it move through the air at high speed.

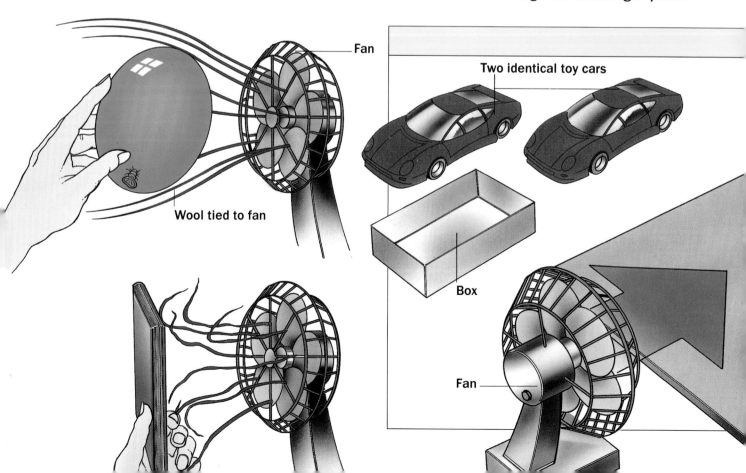

Fan

Wool tied to fan

Two identical toy cars

Box

Fan

DRAG

How much drag an object has depends on its shape. A streamlined object has little drag. A square, unstreamlined object has a lot of drag. This is because when air flows smoothly over a streamlined object, the air does not exert nearly as much force on the object. Another reason for the high drag on unstreamlined objects is that small whirlpools of air form behind an unstreamlined object. The whirlpools, or eddies, lower the air pressure behind the object. This has the effect of holding the object back as it moves along.

▲ Big trucks sometimes have a rounded attachment on the roof of the cab. This allows air to flow smoothly over the truck, reducing drag.

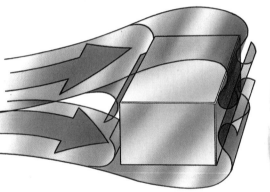

DRAG TEST

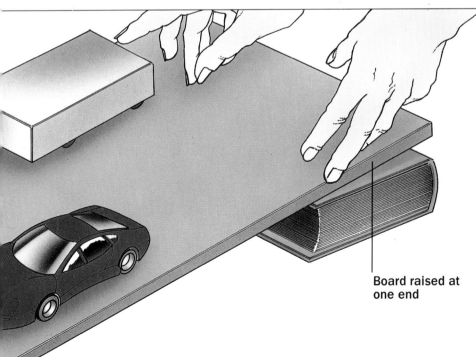

Board raised at one end

You can see the effect of drag if you have two identical toy cars. Cover one with a light cardboard box that does not quite cover the wheels. Put both cars at the top of a sloping board. Which car reaches the bottom first? Repeat the experiment with a fan blowing air at the cars as they roll down the slope. Do the cars take the same time to reach the bottom? Drag depends upon the air speed as well as the shape of a moving object.

We can produce airstreams easily using fans. These airstreams can be controlled and put to work. They can be taken from one place to another using pipes. So, sometimes airstreams are used to control machinery in industry. They are also used to sort out garbage, and to hold hovercraft off the ground.

SORTING GARBAGE

At your local garbage disposal site, the trash is carefully sorted. Some types of garbage are valuable. They can be recycled and used again. Paper, for example, can be shredded and made into paper towels, newspaper and flowerpots. Other waste can be burnt to produce heat energy. Airstreams are used to separate the different types of garbage. The garbage is carried from the tip by a conveyor belt. At the end of the conveyor belt it is dropped into a strong upward current of air. As the garbage falls, the air current carries the lightest material, like paper and cardboard, upwards to be collected for reuse.

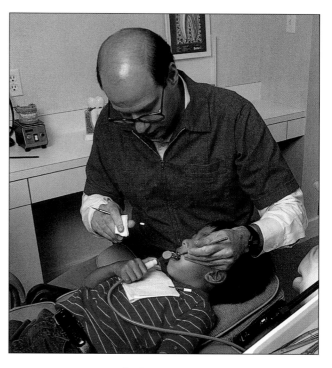

▲ A dentist uses streams of air to suck away waste liquids and keep the patient's mouth clear.

▼ The hovercraft is used in country, like swampland, where normal vehicles cannot go, and for short sea journeys.

FLOATING ON AIR

The hovercraft is called an air-cushion vehicle as it rides on a cushion of air. The air cushion is held in place by a kind of flexible skirt around the base of the craft. A powerful fan forces air into the skirt. The air cannot escape and it lifts the craft off the ground. The hovercraft is driven forward by large propellers at the back. These spin in the air like aircraft propellers. The hull of the hovercraft does not touch the ground as it skims along. This means that it can be used over land, water or swamp. For this reason, hovercraft have been used by explorers in South America and Africa. Hovercraft can travel faster than ships, but they can only be used in calm seas as they overturn easily.

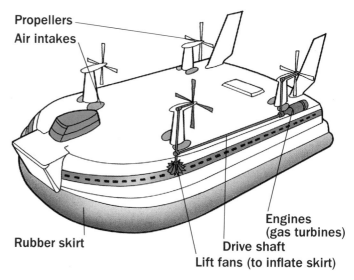

Propellers

Air intakes

Engines (gas turbines)

Rubber skirt

Drive shaft

Lift fans (to inflate skirt)

PAINTING WITH AIR

Streams of air can be used for painting. The first step is to obtain a supply of high-pressure air. This is done with an air compressor, a machine that pumps air into a sealed tank until the pressure builds up. Air, or spray, painting is done with a spray gun. This is attached to the compressed air tank, and to a small container of paint. When the trigger on the spray gun is pressed, air squirts out of a nozzle on the gun. The air flow draws paint from the container and carries it to the object being painted. A spray gun can paint an object in minutes.

▶ Spray painting is used in industry because it produces a smooth surface. It is easy for robot painters to use spray guns.

MAKE A SPRAY GUN

A spray gun can be made with a drinking straw and a plastic pen tube. Fix the pen tube to the straw so that when you blow into the tube, the air stream flows across the top of the straw.

The flow of air across the straw reduces the air pressure in the straw. This draws the paint up the straw and into the air stream. What is the effect of blowing harder into the pen tube?

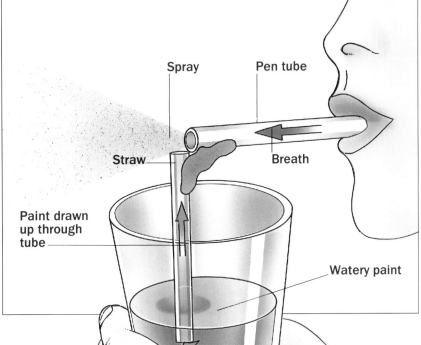

Spray

Pen tube

Straw

Breath

Paint drawn up through tube

Watery paint

WHAT HAPPENS?

If there is a light breeze, what happens if a mixture of corn and chaff are thrown up into the air? The same effect can be seen if you blow on a mixture of corn and chaff held on your hand. This process is called winnowing. It was used by farmers in ancient times to separate corn from unwanted chaff.

Corn and chaff

If there was no air, all objects would fall at the same rate. Light objects would reach the ground side-by-side with heavy objects released at the same time from the same height. However, falling through air is different. Light objects can sometimes fall very slowly. This is why a parachutist can land safely.

FALLING

When something falls through the air, the air slows its fall. There is air resistance, or "drag," on the object. Eventually, the drag slowing a falling object becomes as strong as the pull of gravity which is trying to speed it up. When this happens the speed of the object stays the same. It is said to be moving at its terminal speed. Objects with different shapes have different terminal speeds because the drag is different for different shapes. A person falling with a parachute has a slow terminal speed because the parachute creates lots of drag and so slows his or her fall.

GLIDING THROUGH THE AIR

There are squirrels, lizards, frogs and fish that are skilled gliders. There is even a flying snake which can glide through the air. These animals have folds of skin on each side of their bodies, or on their feet, which they stretch out to form gliding wings. The wings act like parachutes and slow their fall when they leap from high in the treetops. The flying lemur, from the island of Madagascar, is almost helpless on the ground, but it can glide for up to 135 m (440 ft) when it extends the flaps that stretch between its arms and legs. The flying frog has folds of skin between its toes which it extends to make four tiny parachutes. Flying fishes extend fins on the sides of their bodies, and can glide more than 100 yards across the surface of the sea.

▲ Pollen (magnified many times in this photograph) falls to the ground unless carried upwards by air currents.

▼ The flying squirrel, which lives in Africa, can glide 90 m (300 ft) from one tree to another.

FLOATING ON THE AIR

Many living things are able to float on the air. They can do this because they are very light. They also have a large surface area, like a parachute. This means that they can easily float long distances in the air. A dandelion seed may be carried more than 10 km (6 miles) by the wind before landing. Some seeds, such as maple or sycamore seeds, have wings that spin as the seed falls. This helps the seed stay airborne longer.

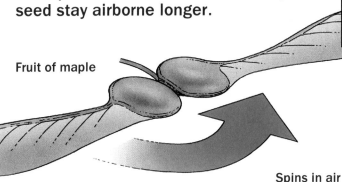

Fruit of maple

Spins in air

▲ A small spider can be carried thousands of miles by its silken parachute. Small spiders have even been found in the air thousands of feet above the Earth's surface.

MAKE A PARACHUTE

Get a square of light cloth, such as an old handkerchief. Cut a circle from the cloth. Tie lengths of string through holes around its edges.

Tie the other ends of the strings to a matchbox with a small weight inside. Cut a hole in the center of the cloth, to let the air flow through it.

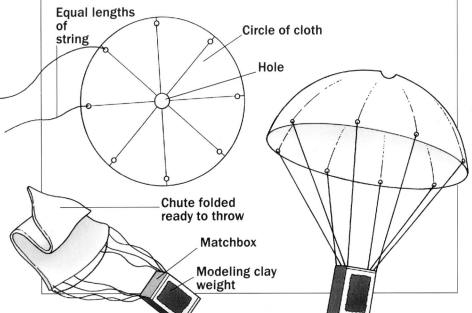

Equal lengths of string

Circle of cloth

Hole

Chute folded ready to throw

Matchbox

Modeling clay weight

WHY?

Why does a dandelion seed have a fluffy head? Why does it need a sudden puff of wind to break the seeds free from the plant? Why are heavier seeds, such as sycamore, elm or pine cones, different?

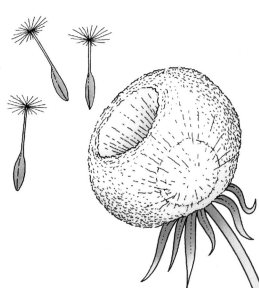

Balloons and blimps float in the air like boats float in water. They are able to do this because their weight is supported by an upwards force called an upthrust, or lift force. The upthrust force is caused by the air pushing on the bottom of the balloon, just like water pushing against the bottom of a floating boat.

EXPANDING AIR

Most things expand, or get bigger, when they are heated. If you heat air in a flexible container, such as a balloon, the air will expand, stretching the balloon. This expansion makes the air in the balloon less dense than the surrounding air. It still weighs the same as it did when cold, but it takes up more space. Because it is taking up more space, it feels a greater upthrust force from the air around it. If the balloon was heated even more, the upthrust might increase sufficiently to lift the balloon from the ground. This is how a hot air balloon rises in the air.

LIGHTER GASES

Some gases, such as helium, are naturally less dense than air. A balloon filled with these gases does not have to be heated to cause lift. In a modern blimp, the lift is provided by a large bag, called the envelope, containing helium. Inside the envelope are small compartments, called ballonets, containing air.

▲ A hot air balloon rises because the warm air inside it is less dense than the surrounding air. This produces a large upthrust force.

Air in a flexible container

Heat expands air making it lighter

Air molecules

Pumping air out of the ballonets decreases the blimp's weight and the blimp rises. Pumping air into the ballonets increases the ship's weight and the ship falls. A blimp also has propellers that drive it through the air.

▲ The propellers, tail fins and rudder on a blimp can be turned to maneuver the blimp when it is moving.

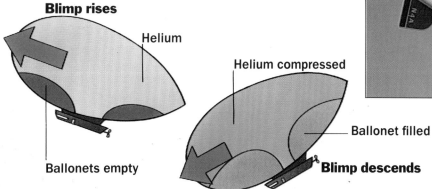

Blimp rises

Helium

Ballonets empty

Helium compressed

Ballonet filled

Blimp descends

THE HOT AIR SCREW

Draw a spiral and aircraft on a circle of cardboard. Cut along the spiral and pull it out a little to make a spiral or coil.

Stand a sharpened pencil on a radiator using modeling clay. Place the coil on the pencil. Watch it turn around.

The coil turns because heated air is rising from the radiator. The current of heated air twists the coil like a propeller.

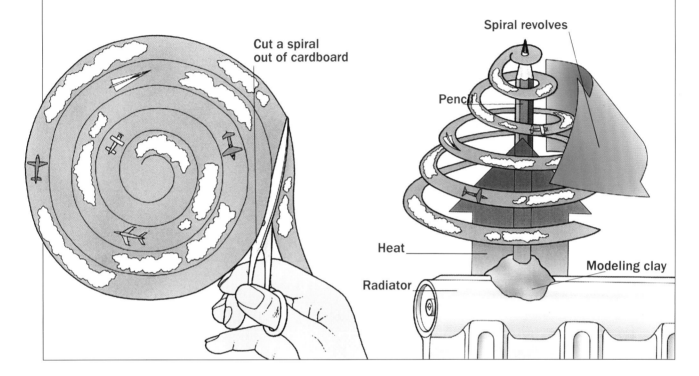

Cut a spiral out of cardboard

Spiral revolves

Pencil

Heat

Radiator

Modeling clay

WHAT HAPPENS?

What happens when an inflated balloon is placed in a warm oven or cupboard and left for half an hour? What happens when the balloon is placed in a refrigerator and left for the same time? Make your experiment more precise by measuring the size around the balloon before placing it in the cupboard or refrigerator and again after taking it out. Does the size of the balloon depend on how long it is in the cupboard or refrigerator or warm oven?

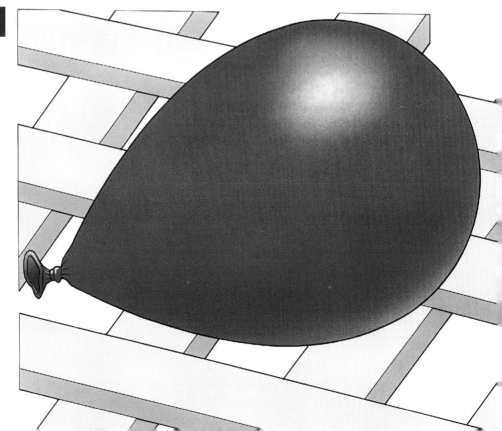

There are many different kinds of flying machines, or aircraft. Some are huge, like the jumbo jet, and some are tiny, like the hang glider. But they all rely on wings to lift them up and keep them aloft. The wings provide an upward force, called "lift," that balances the weight of the aircraft and keeps it in the air.

FLYING WITHOUT POWER

Kites and gliders fly without engine power. They use the forces created by flowing air to provide lift. The wind blows against the kite, which is held at an angle to the wind by the string. The kite deflects the wind downward. As this happens, a reaction force is created on the kite, lifting it up. A hang glider gets its lift in a different way. The triangular glider wing fills with air as the wind blows across it. The wing becomes rounded on top. The air flow around the curved wing produces a force that lifts the glider. A fixed-wing glider like the Space Shuttle also gets its lift from the airflow around its carefully designed wings.

▲ A kite flies steadily in the sky when all the forces acting on it are balanced. The pull on the string is balanced by the wind.

GETTING LIFT

The cross-section of an aircraft wing is a special shape called an airfoil. The airfoil is curved on top and almost flat on the bottom. As the air blows over the wing, or the aircraft moves through the air, the air divides to pass around the wing. The air that passes along the top of the wing moves faster than the air that passes underneath. This is because the air flowing over the top of the wing has further to go, owing to the curved surface of the wing. Fast-moving air has a lower pressure than slow-moving air, so the pressure on the top of the wing is less than the pressure on the bottom. This difference in pressure creates the upwards force called lift. If the aircraft is moving fast enough, the lift is strong enough to support the aircraft.

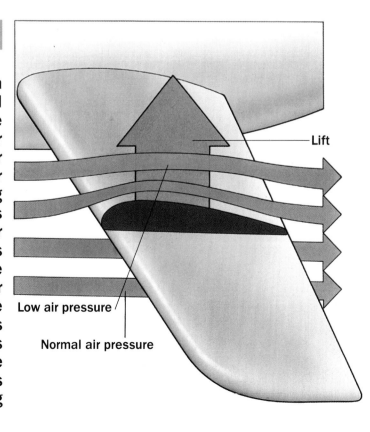

Lift

Low air pressure

Normal air pressure

BIRD LIFT

Birds do more than just flap their wings in order to fly. They also twist the wings, and adjust the angles of the feathers. On the downbeat, the edges of the wing feathers overlap slightly so that no air can pass through them and the wing pushes against the air. On the upbeat, the feathers twist apart so that air can pass through. At the same time, the tips of the wings move in a circle. A forward push of the wingtips on the downstroke propels the bird through the air.

▲ The photograph shows feathers on a bird's wing.

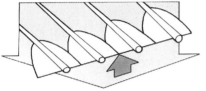

Air resistance closes feathers

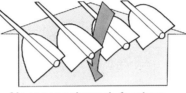

Air passes through feathers

Primary feathers

Upstroke

Downstroke

FAST AIR, LOW PRESSURE

You can see the effect of fast-moving air with a strip of paper. Hold one end of the paper near your mouth and blow. The paper will move upwards and flutter, because the air blowing over its top surface has less pressure than the air beneath it and so has the effect of lifting the paper. Cut small flaps in the end of the strip. Bend one flap down and blow. What happens? Place a small disk of cardboard on a table and see if you can lift it slightly by blowing over the top of it.

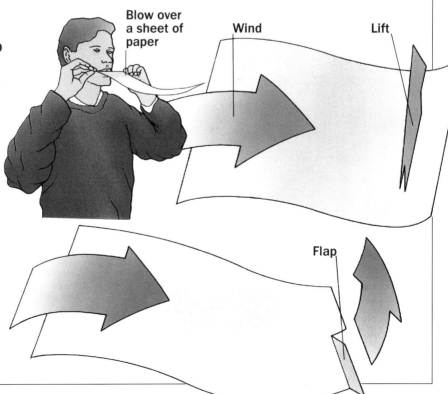

Blow over a sheet of paper

Wind

Lift

Flap

The curved airfoil is put to many different uses. The paradise tree snake from Southeast Asia turns its body into an airfoil when it glides down from a high tree. Throwing sticks and boomerangs, used by some hunting people, are shaped like airfoils to help them fly long distances through the air.

THE HELICOPTER

The helicopter looks very different from other aircraft. Yet, it too gets its lift from airfoils. The whirling rotors have an airfoil shape like the wings of a fixed-wing plane. The difference is that, while a fixed-wing craft has to speed through the air before its wings can lift it up, the rotors of a helicopter produce lift without the craft moving forward. The lift is produced by the airflow over the airfoil-shaped blades as they spin. The airflow around the spinning rotor blades causes low pressure above the blades, which lifts the helicopter.

▲ The angle of a helicopter's blades can be altered to make it move straight up, or forward or backwards. To hover, the speed of the rotors is adjusted.

WING SHAPES

Aircraft have different shapes of wings. A slow-flying glider or light aircraft has long straight wings, which produce high lift at slow speeds. An airliner has swept-back wings which cause less air resistance, or drag, at high speed. However, lift is also reduced so high speeds are needed to take off. A supersonic aircraft, such as Concorde or the Space Shuttle, has dart-shaped or delta wings. This shape reduces drag and helps control the craft at faster-than-sound speeds.

Many aircraft wing shapes have been designed to copy the very effective wing shapes of birds. The long, thin wings of a condor, for example, allows it to soar for hours in search of prey. A hawk has swept-back wings to increase its speed and to allow it to make a sudden dive.

▲ Bats have wings made of skin stretched between thin bones. They are fast and agile fliers.

THE BOOMERANG

The boomerang is a V-shaped throwing stick used for hunting by the Australian aborigines. A boomerang is shaped like an airfoil. Its top surface is rounded and the bottom surface is flat. When the boomerang is thrown, it spins as it moves toward the target. Because of its airfoil shape, the boomerang is lifted as it spins through the air. If the boomerang misses its target, the lift gradually turns the boomerang in a circle so that it returns to the thrower.

▶ Some Australian Aborigines can expertly throw a boomerang to kill game 500 feet away.

MAKE AN AIR-POWERED HELICOPTER

Make two rotor blades by taping a paper strip to two plastic drinking straws. The upper surface of the paper should be curved. Bend one end of the straw so that it points to one side.

Cut two holes in opposite sides of a cardboard tube, sealed at one end. Fix the rotor blades into the holes, using tape. Fix another rotor across the top of the tube.

Blow up a balloon and connect the neck of the balloon to the cardboard tube. When the balloon is released, air will flow through the straws and turn the rotors.

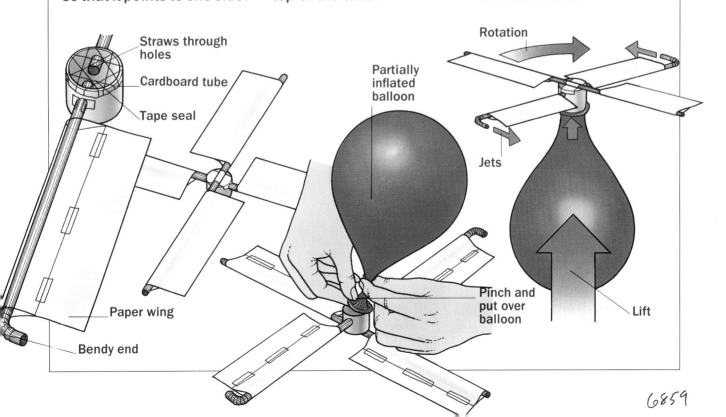

Straws through holes

Cardboard tube

Tape seal

Paper wing

Bendy end

Partially inflated balloon

Pinch and put over balloon

Rotation

Jets

Lift

6859

An aircraft moves through the air because of the forward force, called the thrust, provided by its engines. Sometimes the engine turns a propeller which pushes air backward as it spins, resulting in a forward thrust on the craft. Other aircraft have jet engines which eject a stream of hot gas to produce the thrust.

CONTROLLING AN AIRCRAFT

Flaps on the wings and tail are used to steer an aircraft, and to change its height. Flaps on the back edge of the main wings are called ailerons. These are operated by the pilot moving the control column, or stick, to left or right. The ailerons are connected so that when one goes up, the other goes down. The flaps on the back edge of the tail wings are called elevators. They are also worked by moving the control column. The elevators make the plane climb or dive. The rudder is a flap on the back of the tail. The rudder is used with the ailerons to make a turn.

▲ The direction or height of a hang-glider is altered by changing the position of its wings.

HOW TO STEER

To descend, the pilot of a plane pushes the control column forward. This lowers the elevators on the tail and deflects the airflow so that the tail rises and the nose dips. To climb, a plane pilot pulls the column back. To roll an airplane, the column is moved to one side. This raises one aileron and lowers the other. The wing with the lowered aileron rises and the other wing drops. To turn a plane, the pilot presses the foot pedals to turn the rudder to one side. At the same time, the control column is moved to one side to raise and lower the ailerons.

The controls are different but the effect is the same on a hang glider. The pilot moves the control bar to one side to turn. It is moved forward to climb and backward to dive.

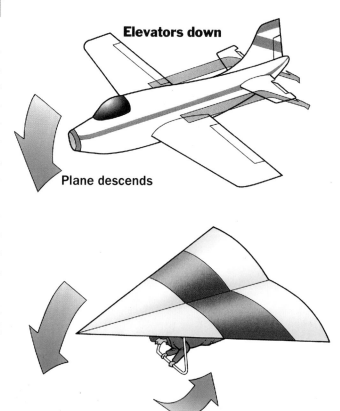

Elevators down

Plane descends

MAKE A SUPER PLANE

Start with a rectangular sheet of paper. Fold it down the center lengthwise. Fold the front edges back twice, to form a triangular shape. Fold the triangular wings out from the body to make the shape shown. This plane should fly well, but to improve its performance, tear a slot at the back and fold it upwards to form a tail. You can make the plane do aerobatics by tearing flaps on the back of the wings. Experiment with the flaps in different positions. How can you make the plane dive, turn, or even loop the loop? How can you make it glide the farthest?

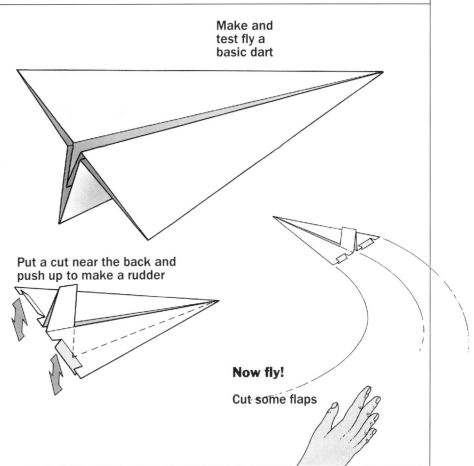

Make and test fly a basic dart

Put a cut near the back and push up to make a rudder

Now fly!

Cut some flaps

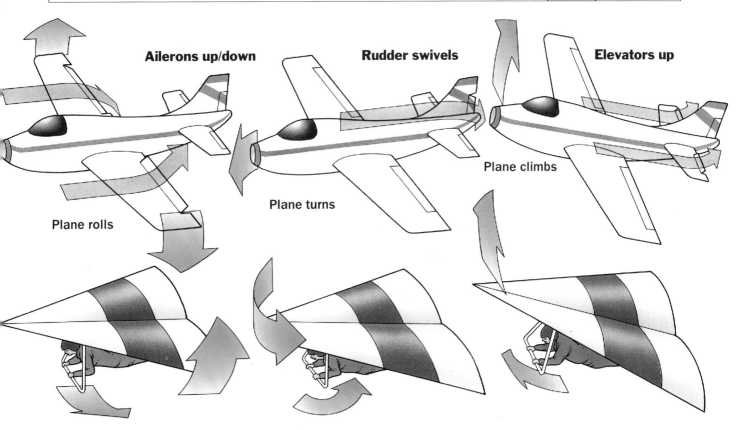

Ailerons up/down

Plane rolls

Rudder swivels

Plane turns

Elevators up

Plane climbs

A fan is used to blow air along, to create a breeze on a hot day, for example. As the blades of the fan turn, they create forces that blow the air forward. But the forces created by the turning blades can be used in other ways. They can pull an aircraft or ship along, and turn machinery, such as electric generators.

THE PROPELLER

Propellers consist of blades attached to a hub which turns. The blades are shaped like airfoils so that when they turn there is less pressure on the curved front surface. This creates a suction force which drags the ship or aircraft forward. Also, as the propeller turns, the blades strike the water or air and push it backward. This produces a forward force, called the reaction force. The reaction force and the suction drive the ship or plane forward. In some propellers, the angle, or pitch, of the blades can be adjusted. At high pitch, the propeller drives the craft forward at speed. The blades can be "feathered" so that they produce little drag when not turning.

▲ The propeller engine is not as powerful or economical as the jet engine. Nevertheless, it is still used on some aircraft.

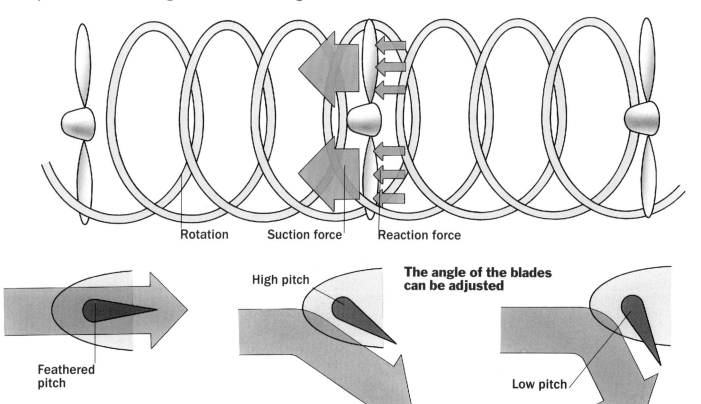

Rotation   Suction force   Reaction force

Feathered pitch

High pitch

The angle of the blades can be adjusted

Low pitch

THE TURBINE

Turbines are a type of engine used to turn electric generators in power stations, ships propellers, and machines in factories. Jet engines which power most large aircraft are a kind of turbine. Inside a turbine, there are two sets of blades. High-pressure steam, water or gas flows over blades, like the blades of a fan or propeller. As the steam, water or gas flows past the blades, it makes them turn. Some are fixed to the shaft and others attached to the casing. This rotation turns the ship's propeller or the electric generator.

▶ Inside a giant turbine used to produce electricity. The blades can be seen. In most power stations, the turbines are turned by steam.

MAKE A PROPELLER-DRIVEN BOAT

Make a propeller by attaching paper blades to the ends of a strong drinking straw. Make sure one side of the blades is curved and the other side is flat, as can be seen in the illustration on the right. Use sticky tape to fix a small cardboard tube to the side of a light, plastic bottle. At the other end of the bottle, attach a bent paper clip. Push a bent paper clip through the center of the straw and join the clips with a rubber band as shown. Attach lollipop sticks to the sides of the bottle, using drinking straws and tape. Wind the propeller to twist the rubber band, and release.

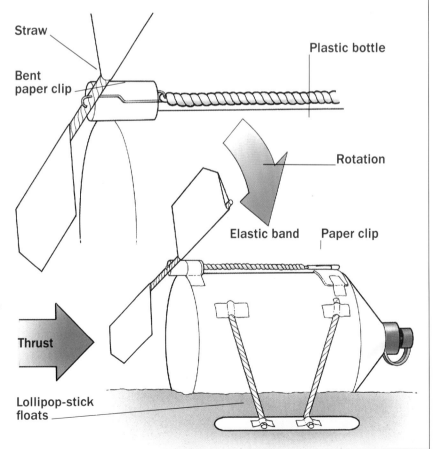

Straw

Bent paper clip

Plastic bottle

Rotation

Elastic band   Paper clip

Thrust

Lollipop-stick floats

Jets and rockets are engines which push aircraft along, rather than pull them through the air using a propeller. In both a jet engine and in a rocket, a stream of hot gases flows from the rear of the engine. As the gases stream out, a thrust or push is developed which drives the engine forward.

THE JET ENGINE

In a jet engine, a fuel such as kerosene is burnt in a combustion chamber. The hot gases escaping from the combustion chamber pass out the rear of the engine, driving the engine forward. As the gases pass out of the engine, they go through a turbine, causing the turbine blades to turn. The blades of the turbine are attached to a shaft. The shaft is connected to another turbine-like device, called a compressor, at the front of the engine. As the compressor is turned by the turbine, the air needed to burn the fuel is drawn into the engines at the front. The compressor squashes, or compresses, the air and forces it at high pressure into the combustion chamber where it burns fiercely.

▲ The jet engine is used in most airliners and military fighters. The photograph shows a side-view of the air-intake and compressor found at the front of a jet engine.

The rear nozzle of a jet engine compresses the escaping gases making them go faster. Putting a cardboard cone around a hair drier has the same effect.

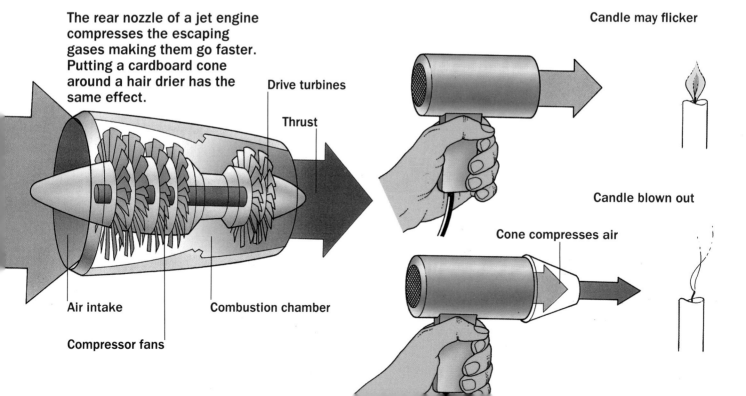

Drive turbines

Thrust

Air intake

Combustion chamber

Compressor fans

Candle may flicker

Candle blown out

Cone compresses air

ROCKETS

The simplest kind of rocket is the firework rocket. Inside the rocket, the explosive fuel burns violently. The gases produced escape from the back of the rocket. Many different fuels are used in space rockets. The most energy-packed is hydrogen. Hydrogen was used to fuel the giant Apollo spacecraft which sent people to the Moon. The oxygen needed to burn the hydrogen is carried in tanks aboard the rocket.

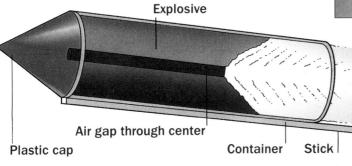

Explosive

Air gap through center

Plastic cap

Container   Stick

▲ An Ariane rocket takes off at the launch site at Kouru in French Guyana. Rockets work in space because they do not need air to burn their fuel.

BALLOON ROCKET

Blow up a long, thin balloon. Put a small tube of cardboard in the neck of the balloon to form a nozzle like on a rocket engine.

Thread string through a drinking straw, and stretch the string across a room. Fix the ends of the string to the walls with adhesive tape.

Fix the drinking straw to the side of the balloon with tape. Hold the balloon at one end of the room and let go of the nozzle.

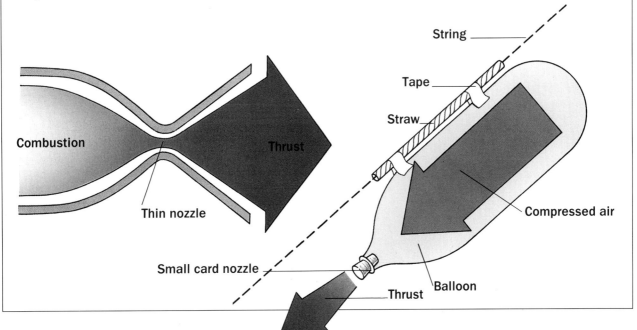

Combustion

Thin nozzle

Thrust

String

Tape

Straw

Compressed air

Small card nozzle

Thrust

Balloon

People have always dreamed of flying in the skies. According to one ancient Greek myth, the first people to fly were Daedalus and his son Icarus. In the myth, they flew from Crete to the island of Santorini using wings made of wax and feathers. Icarus flew too close to the Sun. His wings melted and he fell into the sea.

Icarus attempts to fly

The first successful flight was in a hot air balloon. It was sent up in 1783 by two French brothers, Joseph and Etienne Montgolfier. The balloon carried three passengers, a sheep, a cockerel, and a duck. After a short flight, the animals landed safely. It was Englishman Sir George Cayley who first made a glider with wings and a tail like the airplanes of today. In 1853, he launched into the air carrying his coachman. Afterwards, the frightened man told his employer, "Please, Sir George, I wish to resign. I was hired to drive horses, not to fly."

The first successful powered flight was made by the Wright brothers in 1903.

The Wright brothers, Orville and Wilbur, invented and built the first successful powered airplane. The historic first flight took place on a freezing cold morning on 17 December 1903 at Kitty Hawk in North Carolina. With Orville at the controls, their craft remained aloft for just over 12 seconds. It flew a distance of 36 m (120 ft). Later in the day they made much longer flights. Their machine, called *Flyer*, was only 6 m (20 ft) long, and could only carry the pilot. It had two propellers driven by a chain from the engine. Within two years the Wright brothers' machine could fly 40 km (24 miles) in 38 minutes.

The Montgolfier brothers launched the first hot air balloon in 1783.

In 1988 the old myth about Icarus came true. A Greek, called Kanellos Kanellopoulos, flew the 118 km (73 miles) from Crete to Santorini entirely under his own power. There was no motor in his aircraft, which was named *Daedalus* after the mythical Greek flyer. The strange-looking craft was made of strong and light carbon fibers and thin plastic sheeting. It had wings 35 m (114 ft) across. The pilot, sitting in the cabin, pedaled to turn a large propeller at the front. The aircraft was slow moving. It only reached a speed of 29 km/h (18 mph), and flew at a height of 4.5 m (15 ft) above the sea. Had Kanellopoulos crashed, like Icarus, his fall would have been cushioned by the sea. It seems the wish to fly like a bird is as strong today as it was in Ancient Greece.

Aileron
A movable flap at the rear edge of an aircraft wing near the tip. The aileron controls the rolling movements of the aircraft.

Airfoil
A surface, like an aircraft wing, which is shaped to produce lift when air flows over and under it.

Air pressure
The downward pressure of the atmosphere. It is caused by the weight of the air.

Air resistance
The slowing force, also called drag, which resists the movement of an object through the air.

Anemometer
An instrument used for measuring the speed of the wind.

Anticyclone
An area of high atmospheric pressure, from which winds blow outward.

Atmosphere
The layer of air that surrounds the Earth.

Beaufort scale
A scale used to measure the strength of winds. The scale is named after Francis Beaufort, a British commander who developed it.

Depression
An area of low air pressure toward which winds blow. Warm areas tend to have a low pressure.

Drag
The resistance of the air or water to the movement of anything, such as an aircraft, ship or car, through it.

Elevator
A flap on the rear wings of an aircraft that is moved to make the craft climb or dive.

Gravity
The force that draws any two bodies together. Gravity causes objects to have weight by attracting them to the Earth.

Isobar
A line on a map that connects places having the same air pressure at a given time.

Jet engine
A type of engine used in most large aircraft. A stream of hot gases is expelled from the rear of the engine, driving the aircraft forward.

Lift
A force that pushes an object, such as a boat or aircraft, upward.

Rudder
A moveable flap at the back of an aircraft's tail which is used to turn the craft.

Streamlining
Making an object smooth and rounded so that air or water flows easily over it.

Terminal speed
The constant speed which falling objects reach when falling through a gas or a liquid.

Thrust
The force produced by an engine, which drives it forward.

Turbine
An engine which is turned by a flow of gas or water directed through the blades of a kind of fan.

Photographic Credits:
Cover: Zefa; pages 7, 8, 9l, 10b, 18 both, 24 and 26: Rovert Harding Library; pages 9r, 13 and 22t: Chapel Picture Library; pages 10t, 12, 16b, 17, 21, 22b, and 23: Bruce Coleman Ltd; page 11: R.W. Munro Ltd.; pages 14 and 16t: Science Photo Library; page 15: GEC; page 27: CEGB; page 28: Rolls-Royce; page 29: ESA; page 30t: Mary Evans Picture Library; page 30b: Popperfoto.